BMW
R69 & R69S

Roy Harper

CONTENTS

Foulis

Haynes

Further titles in this series will be published at
regular intervals. For information on new titles
please contact your bookseller or write to the
publisher.

ISBN 0 85429 387 6

A FOULIS Motorcycling Book

First published 1983

© **Haynes Publishing Group**

Published by:
Haynes Publishing Group
Sparkford, Yeovil,
Somerset BA22 7JJ

Distributed in USA by:
Haynes Publications Inc.
861 Lawrence Drive, Newbury
Park, California 91320, USA

Editor: Jeff Clew
Dust jacket design: Rowland Smith
Page Layout: Michael King
Colour photography: Andrew Morland
Road tests: Courtesy of *Motor Cycling*
and *Motor Cycle* (IPC)
Printed in England by: J.H.Haynes &
Co. Ltd

This book is dedicated to

E. J. (Ted) Davies
who likes them fast

FOREWORD

Shareholders were shocked. Their firm was going bankrupt! At a heated annual general meeting in 1959, bankers suggested that share values should be halved and the company sold – possibly to the Solex Carburettor Company or to Daimler-Benz. Fortunately for BMW, Dr. Herbert Quandt, an influential major shareholder, led a successful rescue operation. He managed to persuade the bankers to postpone their decision, inaugurated changes on the board and backed the manufacture of small cars fitted with motorcycle engines.

These cars (BMW 700s) became popular, the company flourished, and in 1963 the loyal shareholders even received dividends – the first for 20 years!

Meanwhile, the R69, introduced in 1955, had become firmly established with discerning motorcyclists, and was to continue in production until 1969. It was replaced with a new generation of 'Bee-ems' that has continued to satisfy those riders who 'want something better' despite the blandishments of rival 'superbikes' covered in gewgaws.

The R69 is rightly held in great esteem throughout the world, and this Super Profile is an affectionate, but objective, cameo of this popular model – tracing the reliable BMW's design and development right back to its roots in the very first transverse flat twin BMW – the R32 born 60 years ago.

The enthusiasm of BMW owners has made the research for this little book a real pleasure and I should like to thank Fred Secker, Bruce Preston, Margaret Clarke and Ted Davis of the BMW Club for

their kind assistance; also *Motor Cycle Weekly* and *Motorcycle Sport* for permission to use road tests and articles; Frank Cox and John Frith for lending their motorcycles; and finally my long-suffering secretary, Jan Williamson, who managed to decipher my scribbles to type the manuscript.

Roy Harper

HISTORY & EVOLUTION

The legendary First World War fighter ace, Freiherr Manfred von Richthofen, owed much of his success in the air to the reliability and power of his engine, which had been designed and manufactured by Karl Rapp and Max Friz.

Rapp had started his firm, Rapp Motorenwerke Munchen GmbH, in 1913 to produce aeroplane engines and three years later he decided to merge with Gustav Otto Flugmotorenfabrik (aircraft makers) to form Bayerische Flugzeugwerke AG. His fellow director was a brilliant designer named Dr Ing E Max Friz. So good were their engines that they attracted the attention of an Austrian engineer, Franz Popp, who promptly arrived at the door to enquire if they could use some Austrian wherewithal. They welcomed Popp and his money and sat him on the board as Managing Director of a new company, Bayerische Motoren Werke AG, which commenced trading in 1917. In 1918 the firm went public with stock capital of 12 million Reichsmarks and no less than 3,500 employees. Within a year, Friz had to stop production of his beloved aero engine because such interesting projects were banned by the Treaty of Versailles. However, clandestine research resulted in a new world altitude record for an aircraft – a BMW-engined aeroplane was piloted to 32,030 feet. Members of the Allied Commission of Control were furious and forbade any more research.

So it was back to earth for Friz to manufacture mundane articles like hefty agricultural items. Coming down to earth was all very well but this was ridiculous.

Friz looked around for other products to make. Motorcycles were unappealing to him but the public liked them and therein lay salvation. A little 148 cc 2-stroke was produced, but what to call this first two-wheeler to carry the BMW badge? The company wanted a name, a resounding name that would become a household word. So they called the bike the Flink.

The Flink came, aroused little enthusiasm in Friz, and departed unlamented. The next effort was the Helios, which incorporated a new engine, the M2B15, a two-cylinder air-cooled horizontally-opposed side valve installed lengthways. This was fine for cooling the front cylinder but not so cool for the one sited aft. With a 5 to 1 compression ratio this 500 cc engine developed $6\frac{1}{2}$ bhp at 2,800 rpm and was used by various manufacturers before it appeared in the Helios. Douglas had used a similar type of engine for more than a decade quite successfully, despite the commonly-held belief that engine seizures were inevitable due to the rear cylinder overheating. In point of fact this was untrue. The direction of rotation of the engine caused more oil to reach the rear cylinder and help it to run cooler, whereas the front cylinder was often in a calm air pocket, masked by the front wheel and mudguard.

Even so, Friz reverted to a transverse layout like that of the ABC, and produced the R32 in 1923. This model was important for it established the basic design on which later BMW motorcycles were to be constructed. Gone was the rear chain in favour of shaft drive, while the clutch and gearbox were akin to those of a car. These components were housed in a new duplex tubular frame which gave greater lateral and torsional rigidity than hitherto. The engine, (now designated M2B33) had been developed to produce $8\frac{1}{2}$ bhp at 3,300 rpm and propelled the bike at the steady rate of 55 mph. Over 3,000 were produced until production ceased in 1926.

Meanwhile, various ohv models were designed and built, culminating in 1928 with the 750 cc ohv-engined R63. This churned out 24 bhp and achieved an impressive 75 mph. An eager record chaser, Ernst Henne, decided this new motor was the finest thing since pneumatic tyres and became an habitual breaker of world records, smashing the world 2-wheel land speed record 8 times in just 8 years, and taking the 3-wheel record twice *en passant* by adding another wheel to his BMW. His last solo record (173.67 mph) was set in 1937 and survived until 1951!

In between breaking world records, Henne competed in various races, trials and hill climbs for BMW, riding a variety of their current motorcycles. The pressed steel frame was introduced for some machines and the production models included side valve or overhead valve models of 200, 250, 300, 350, 400, 500, 600 and 750 cc, the last named being fitted with hydraulically-damped telescopic front forks in 1935. The German army used BMW motorcycles extensively during the Second World War and this helped the firm maintain profitability. (An interesting project was the building of a jet engine in 1943.) When Germany had been defeated and divided East and West, the Russian zone included the Eisenach works where all BMW cars had been made. The Munich works had been knocked about by allied bombers and the Spandau plant in Berlin had also been bombed. It was under the control of the Russians who stripped it of useful equipment.

Prohibited from making

5

motorcyles, the skilled BMW engineers suddenly found they were culinary consultants producing a range of cooking pots and pans. Then restrictions were eased in 1946 and motorcycle production was allowed to proceed.

By 1948 BMW were really back in business with a useful two-fifty (the R24) akin to the popular war-time bike, the R23. (This ohv single produced 10 bhp at 5,400 rpm and 8,000 were made from 1938 till 1941). Over 12,000 R24s were made during an 18 month period ending in 1950 with a revised version, the R25.

Later that year, when restrictions on cubic capacity were lifted, BMW announced the R51/2. Although this ohv 494 cc transverse-engined mount obviously owed its genesis to the 1938 R51, the big news for the BMW boys was that the twin was back. It could not compete with the Ariel Square Four or the Vincent Vee twin but its breeding offered the devotees reliability and quietness, while the sober black enamel gave dignity. This model was superseded in 1952 by the R51/3 which incorporated a greatly revised engine although output was the same – 24 bhp at 5,800 rpm.

Of greater interest to us is the appearance the same year of the R67 which incorporated a new 590 cc engine, a tuned version of which would be the heart of the R69. This model could give the Ariel a good run, should they every meet! This was rare, as few Ariels were sold to Germany while BMW had difficulty penetrating the UK market due to the high cost – the R67 was dearer than any UK roadster. By the mid '50s, when the R67 and its derivative, the faster R68 (reputedly the first BMW to do the ton), were phased out, the post-war boom in big motorcycles had tailed off. (Vincents ceased production in 1955 and Ariels followed shortly after.) While P.C. Vincent in England was trying, in vain, to keep alive the legendary 1000 cc vee-twins by cladding his 9-year-old

engine in fibreglass panels, BMW tried to stay solvent by distracting enthusiasts' attention from the antiquated design of their transverse engines by offering a new frame and forks.

Devotees are a conservative group and not only eschew change for its own sake. Many dislike *any* change, loving their bikes – faults and all. It is interesting the way in which followers of different marques identify with the model of their choice and maintain that the works went downhill when their particular model was dropped from the range. And an awful lot of models were dropped by many manufacturers going broke, especially the makers of sidecars.

Interest in sidecars waned. Few riders could resist swapping the 'combo' for one of the many cheap mass-produced family saloons coming on to the market. Although BMW produced cars, they were not holding a large enough share of the market to remain profitable. BMW therefore wanted to boost sales of motorcycles (as well as cars) with new ideas, while avoiding frightening off the traditionalists. This was achieved by building a new range of motorcycles around the old engines with new cycle parts.

The 1955 front end consisted of Earles forks (originally designed by an Englishman, Ernest Earles) in which the main tubes swept back and down to the pivot with the long leading links. Movement was controlled by spring and damper units. Duplex down tubes ran from the steering head beneath the power unit and back to the rear wheel before curving gracefully up to the single top tube. Each rear swinging arm pivoted on a near vertical tube (set in the curve) cross-braced just above and below the pivot. The pair of spring/damper units could be adjusted to suit the weight of a pillion passenger. (A girl friend once complained that she was merely regarded as the ballast keeping the rear wheel down.)

The right arm of the trailing

forks housed the previously exposed final drive shaft; the wheel size was reduced from 19 inches to 18 and the front brake now boasted twin leading shoes.

The engine of the R69 was basically the 600 cc unit of the R68, which in turn was a more powerful version of the R67 (which traced its ancestry back to the pre-war era). Bore and stroke were 72 x 73 mm, giving 594 cc, and output with a compression ratio of 8 to 1 was 35 at 6,800 rpm, resulting in a road speed of around 'the ton'. The camshaft was located directly above the crankshaft from which it was driven via a pair of helical gears. The crankshaft also drove the oil pump via gears and the dynamo, with which the magneto was snugly encased in a one-piece alloy casting. The crankshaft ran on roller big-ends and was supported by ball bearing mains. The connecting rods carried aluminium pistons within iron barrels on which were mounted light alloy cylinder heads. These (with their valves) were housed in smart alloy covers with each head fed by a 26 mm Bing carburettor. Unusually, efficiency gave way to aesthetic requirements – the oil orifice was tucked away behind a cylinder and some ham-fisted riders poured more oil outside the filler than within. (Not that the oil-tight engine needed much replenishing.) The left-hand foot change for the four-speed gearbox was the reverse of the usual layout of English motorcycles but the latter eventually adopted the continental arrangement. The R69 engine incorporated a new (diaphragm) clutch and new four-speed gearbox – the engine was flexible enough to obviate more – but shifting gear was still a leisurely, noisy business compared to the quiet snappy changes available to riders of British machines of equivalent performance. The engine was economical – touring around 60-70 mph gave 60-70 mpg, depending on how heavy handed was the rider. BMWs had to be good to justify their price in England, for example, where at £400 they were almost twice the price of their BSA or Triumph equivalents on display at Earls Court in 1955.

About the time of the 1955 Motor Cycle Show, Sheldon, an authority on veteran and vintage motorcycles, pointed out that 50 years had elapsed since a man named Barter had visited the editor of *The Motor Cycle* in London. He had ridden from Bristol on a push-bike fitted with his own square (55.5 mm bore and stroke) flat-twin engine clipped lengthways between the front down tube and the seat tube, probably the first practical use of a horizontally-opposed engine. The $2\frac{1}{2}$ hp device was capable of 20 mph 'but the great charm of the machine was its quiet and practically vibration-free running', a description which could equally be applied to the BMWs of 1955. Unlike Douglas, who took over the manufacture of Barter's bike in 1907, BMW did not take a stand at the Show but ensured that it would be part of the scene by hitching an R67/3 to a TR500 sidecar on the Steib stand. (The bike did not boast the new rear frame and Earles forks.)

Bruce Preston began his BMW ownership with a 1953 R67/2 and thought it was the best outfit he ever rode, with a top speed of around 75 mph and yielding 50 mpg. He reckoned the compression ratio of 6.5 to 1 was so low that the engine could be started by hand. Anyway, BMW entered Bruce's bloodstream and is still there a quarter of a century later.

BMW's failure to advertise one of their new 'Earles' models at the main show of the year in the United Kingdom is surprising (attendance on the first day alone was over 64,000!) especially as they had displayed their new range at the Brussels show during the first half of 1955.

BMW continued to offer the R67/3 – with its outdated plunger system – for sidecar use for several

months until the introduction of its successor, the R60, in 1956. This model featured Earles forks and swinging arm, like the new 500 cc machine, the R50, with whom it shared common cycle parts, gearbox and clutch, etc. The 595 cc engine of the R60 produced 28 bhp at 5,600 rpm with a compression ratio of 6.5 to 1, compared to the R50's 26 bhp at 5800 rpm.

Bruce Preston (a Vice-President of the BMW Club) has owned an R60 for years, travelled to work on it, done the Exeter, and thrashed it around Silverstone with an anguished chair which finally expired near the pits – the intrepid passenger had made the mistake of standing up in the sidecar only to go straight through the remains of the floor. 'Don't just stand there', bawled Bruce, 'Run!'

A new R60 cost £390 in 1956, the R50 was £378, the R69 a hefty £492 5s 7d, and completing the Earles-fork range, the little R26, a 245 cc single that must have been the most luxurious two-fifty yet made with its comfortable suspension, shaft drive and superb finish (hence the asking price of £256).

The BMW single had been pretty successful – sales for the two decades of production totalled 167,365 motorcycles, the prices being appreciably higher than those of BSA twins of double the capacity and having almost twice the performance. In 1955, for the price of a BMW two-fifty (£228), it was possible to choose instead a BSA B34 Competition model, an AJS, Matchless, Norton or Royal Enfield five-hundred, the famous Triumph Speed Twin or a Velocette MSS.

Yet it was a difficult time for motorcycle manufacturers. BMW sales in 1957 slumped to 25 per cent of the 1954 total and many famous marques disappeared from motorcycle trade fairs.

Many motorcyclists of that era regarded a bike as a stepping stone to four wheels, and quadrupeds – often in extraordinary guises – were very cheap indeed.

There were flimsy mobile metal cans recommended by famous personages grinning their encouragement. (A cynic suggested that the famous grins were stimulated not by the gimmicky cars but by the size of the cheques.) Anyway, BMW got into the act by installing motorcycle engines in lightweight cars but their financial position deteriorated and ended in the controversial AGM of 1959.

The company was now very vulnerable. The big cars were not 'moving', as the showroom salesmen succinctly put it, and a world-wide bias against motorcycles generally had hit the sales of the two-wheelers, especially the big 'uns. The future of the main spheres of activity – the reliable aeroplane engines, the unpopular cars of quality and the world-renowned motorcycles – now rested on a small saloon car fitted with a motorcycle engine. Fortunately, the 700, introduced in 1959, had the advantage of a reliable, efficient, rear-mounted, rear-drive engine which produced 30 bhp at 4800 rpm. The engine was ripe for tuning. A more powerful version (700CS and LS) produced 32 bhp at 5000 rpm in 1961 and from this modest beginning the little car spawned sporting offspring that developed 70 bhp at 8000 rpm and showed their paces against the ubiquitous Mini that was also born in 1959, soon to be hotted up for rallies and races.

After the difficulties of 1959, the 700 (the Cabrio version was capable of 85 mph) added almost five million marks to the sales figures during 1960, just enough to keep the company going until the new BMW 1500 car arrived in 1961, to prove both popular and profitable, enabling the firm to pay a dividend in 1963.

Meanwhile, the sports version of the R69 which had appeared in 1960, appealed to an ever-increasing band of motorcycle enthusiasts, who appreciated the bike's ability to take them vast distances across Europe's open highways which were then free from speed limits.

Fast though the riders and bikes were, their image was of unhurried, courteous travel, in welcome contrast to the 'ton up kids' who, as 'rockers' astride fast light machines up to 650 cc, vied with scooter mounted 'mods' at various resorts. If 'yobbos' have ever owned BMWs, I have yet to meet one. The price alone was enough to deter the usual 'cafe racer'. In spring 1960 the purchase of the R69 in Britain left little change out of £500 – enough perhaps for a new helmet and gloves. When the new R69S arrived in Britain a month before Christmas, £530 had to be found – nearly twice the price of a British bike with equal speed, snappier gear changing and superior road holding for 'ear holing'.

For the extra money, the BMW enthusiast, who typically kept the same machine for several seasons, enjoyed, for example, the quality of complex castings and expensive forgings while the rear main bearing was designed to cope with flexure of the crankshaft. The finish was of superb quality – be it the sober dignified black enamel with white lines or the reverse colour scheme. In 'pre-Jap' days the weight of the 600 cc R69S was against it – about four cwt, the same as the faster, cheaper Vincent vee-twin and Ariel Square Four (both defunct by the sixties and selling second-hand for less than £200).

With a top speed of 110 mph, the R69S was the fastest production BMW yet produced, with 42 bhp at 7000 rpm on hand and a compression ratio of 9.5 to 1. Whereas sales of the R69 were only 2819 machines from 1955-60, 11,417 examples of the R69S were sold during the decade of its production. (Then, for the seventies, the works embarked on a totally new range to compete successfully with the Jap superbikes.)

Until the sixties, BMW's attitude had been that riders were not sold BMW motorcycles – they bought them. (Or rather, they used to. Sales of motorcycles had fallen. Impressed by the success of their various cars, the management was inclined to wind up motorcycle manufacture altogether). Aggressive selling methods were the antithesis of the BMW philosophy. However, when Japanese bikes threatened traditional markets, BMW altered its attitude and adopted a very positive marketing strategy.

They had a good base to build on. Badge loyalty meant a great deal to devotees ... and total sales of bikes of various makes in the USA and elsewhere were rising.

But what sort of motorcyclist was handing over wads of hard-earned dollars to be part of this expanding new sport, to know the thrills of the wind parting his hair at the ton with a loyal girl clinging to his waist, to suffer spills that taught him his limits or to experience mechanical breakdown miles from home until, exhausted from pushing inanimate metal that appeared to double in weight every mile, he was ready to sell the bike for the first proffered buck?

The modern motorcyclist wanted such unheard-of refinements as electric starting, indicators telling him which way he was turning, notification of the gear in use and required that the engine used the oil it was fed for lubricating essential moving parts instead of the highway or his clothes. And if his bike was decked out with impressive gewgaws and gimmicks, so much the better for the image.

These requirements made the benign Bee-em look somewhat staid and the R69 and its smaller brother, the 494 cc R50, were dropped by BMW despite being part of the best-looking range ever made by them.

Out went the old heave-ho of kickstarting. Out went Henry Ford's dictum, 'You can have any colour

so long as it's black'. Out went the old frame and Earles forks ... and in came the /5 series with new engines, frames and colour. But that era is another story: unfinished, I'm pleased to say!

Road racing and world records

The R69 was never meant to be used for scratching round race circuits. However, it would not be unkind or untrue to say that BMW designed a twin engine for the 1923 R32 and that all their subsequent twin cylinder motorcycle engines have been but variations on a basic theme, be they side valve, overhead valve or overhead cam. This brief racing history therefore covers a selection of the exploits of the twin engine ending, appropriately, with a specially-prepared R69 attacking records at Montlhéry.

The first BMW transverse flat twin, the R32, was winning races almost as soon as its existence was known. The machine, made by Stolle and Bieber from the design by Friz, was raced by Bieber in 1924 and the same year was good enough to win him the national championship, a title held by 500 cc BMWs for the next eight years.

To assist the racing men, a few R37 production machines were tuned for competition and incorporated an alloy cylinder head designed by Rudolf Schleicher, a shorter wheelbase and strengthened front forks. Supercharging was introduced in 1926 and gave BMW riders the advantage on the straights, but the riders of English machines, which could nip round corners more quickly, passed them on the bends.

Work entries ceased in 1930, but not before BMW had achieved nearly 100 impressive wins, including the Targa Florio three times.

However, BMW were back five years later with a new (supercharged) 500 cc machine ridden by 'Wiggerl' Kraus at Berlin.

The flat twin engine incorporated two overhead camshafts to each cylinder with one timing shaft driving both, the Zoller blower running off the front of the crankshaft. Kraus did not win but he proved the reliability of the engine and when the bike was harnessed to a new plunger frame in 1936, it was almost unbeatable.

Various manufacturers, including Vincents, Nortons and Moto-Guzzi, had shown the advantage of a sprung back end over a rigid frame (which left a rider feeling he had been 'worked over' by the boys) – a rider could actually leap off the bike after losing a race and trot away to the beer tent; and BMW riders such as Karl Gall and Otto Ley were soon clearing out their cabinets to make room for silver trophies. Jock West, the first Englishman to ride a works BMW, joined the act and won the Ulster Grand Prix in 1937 and 1938.

Georg Meier won the European championship for BMW in 1938 and a year later became the first alien to win the Senior TT. For good measure, his team mate, Jock West, came second. Then came the war and a long interlude before Germany was defeated in 1945 and finally allowed back into the FIM in 1951, the first race being at Schotten. The old duo of BMW and Meier was back and won, but the all-conquering Nortons led by Geoff Duke won the major prizes.

Although BMW failed to win any major solo titles in the 1950s it achieved successes in the Barcelona 24 hours and the Thruxton 500 and was almost unbeatable in the sidecar class. The first significant win came in 1951 at Hockenheim, when Kraus and Huser beat the reigning world champions, Oliver and Dobelli (Norton). 1954 saw the start of BMW's long domination of the world sidecar championship (although there was no official manufacturer's title that year) beginning with Noll and Cron and ending in 1974 with Kraus (BMW

failing to win the title just twice). Thereafter 500 cc two-strokes reigned supreme.

Meanwhile, BMW attacked various world records, starting with the eight and nine hour records at Montlhéry on 12th May, 1954. The works team set a new average speed of 103 mph using the RS 500 fitted with an aluminium fairing up front. At the end of October, Wilhelm Noll arrived at the same track to set a new record of 132 mph over 10 kilometres. In March, 1955, Noll was joined by two other successful sidecar drivers, Hillebrand and Schneider, and they averaged 89 mph at Montlhéry over 24 hours to collect yet another record for BMW.

Using the autobahn near Munich on October 5th, Walter Zeller smashed the 10 kilometre standing start record with a speed of 150 mph and the 10 mile record with 147 mph.

Wilhelm Noll then beat the world sidecar record of 162 mph (set earlier in the year by Bob Burns on a Vincent) with a speed of 174 mph. (Within a year, Burns beat Noll's speed riding a Vincent Black Lightning at Utah, USA.)

The company ceased financing world record attempts but several records were broken during the next two decades by privately tuned BMWs, notably by Jack Forrest in New South Wales, Australia. In 1957, using a streamlined BMW five-hundred, he set a new record of 149 mph, a figure that also beat the previous best times for 750 and 1000 cc two-wheelers.

In 1956 at Montlhéry, J. Murit averaged 109 mph to beat the 100 mile and 1 hour sidecar record. At Monza in 1958, Florian Camathias averaged 120.7 mph over the 100 kilometre distance for a new sidecar record and followed this a few weeks later (at Charat) with a new sidecar record of 95.4 mph for the one kilometre standing start.

An R69S was taken to Montlhéry in 1961 to attack the 12

and 24 hour records. Munich tuned the engine, which was installed in a bike prepared by the MLG firm of London. The highly geared bike incorporated various non-standard items including extra lamps, a Peel fairing and racing saddle. To give the boys added comfort as they stretched out (or perhaps crouched in), the petrol tank was padded. The team of Sid Mizen, John Holder, George Catlin and Ellis Boyce set a new average speed of 109 mph for both the 12 and 24 hours.

The success of the R69

'To travel hopefully is a better thing than to arrive', wrote Robert Louis Stevenson, possibly referring to a visit to his mother-in-law, 'and the true success is to labour', perhaps recalling occasions when the mechanical contrivances of the nineteenth century failed to labour long enough.

Stevenson's namesake, who built the first steam locomotive, the *Rocket*, would have approved of the BMW and admired its longevity and low-revving engine compared to cheaper, brash products from lesser manufacturers. Certainly, there is no engine in production as vibration-free as the flat-twin. Judged as an efficient piece of engineering, the BMW is a success, notwithstanding its recordbreaking.

It commands a loyal band of riders, including those who feel that the only true BMWs were made *before* 1970. As a motorcycle, therefore, it is a success.

Yet what is the verdict of the market place? The R69 and R69S were designed during the mid-fifties when motorcycling was in a profitless hiatus between the early post-war years – when motorcycles were bought as daily transport – and the sixties, when two-wheelers were increasingly purchased for pleasure, especially the 500 to 1000 cc range which was, of course, BMW's forte. This social phenomenon is reflected in the sales figures. From 1955 to 1960, only 2,819 R69 bikes were sold, whereas sales of the R69S from 1960 until 1969 totalled 11,417. The sidecar market was still profitable and to cater for it BMW offered the R60, of which 20,828 examples were sold. (With its engine's low state of tune – for example, 6.5 to 1 compression ratio compared to the R69's 8 to 1 – the R60 also appealed, as a flexible tourer, to solo riders for whom the works fitted a higher ratio rear axle.) As a commercial proposition, these figures were acceptable, so in the market place the BMW can be judged a success.

But what of fashion? Oscar Wilde pointed out that one should never be too modern or one would suddenly be old-fashioned. BMW have never changed anything

unless absolutely necessary – they finally introduced disc brakes long after many rivals fitted them as standard. As a result of this conservative attitude, spares were interchangeable – all the basic models produced between 1955 and 1969 used identical frame parts, to the benefit of the owners, unlike the position today with some Japanese manufacturers who change components so frequently that it is difficult and expensive for dealers and riders to obtain spares.

While the Japanese dominate world markets with their small capacity motorcycles, BMW continue to appeal to the hard-riding tourer with their range of fast, expensive machines. In a world recession, that is success indeed.

SPECIFICATION

R69 and R69S models

Model	R69	R69S
Engine		
Two cylinders horizontally opposed		
Type number	268/2	268/3
Bore and stroke mm	72 x 73	72 x 73
Cubic capacity	590	590
Compression ratio	8:1	9.5:1
Valve arrangement	ohv	ohv
Carburettors	Bing (2)	Bing (2)
bhp	35 @ 6800 rpm	42 @ 7000 rpm
Coresponding bmep kg/cm^2	7.96	9.28
Oil capacity in litres (pints)	2 ($3\frac{1}{2}$)	2 ($3\frac{1}{2}$)
Transmission		
Type number	245/1	245/1
Gear ratios – Bottom	3.46:1	3.46:1
Second	1.96:1	1.96:1
Third	1.32:1	1.32:1
Top	1:1	1:1
Final drive ratio	3.18 or 4.25:1	3.13 or 4.33:1
Frame		
Tubular loop		
Type Number	245/1	245/2*
Front forks	Earles	†Earles
damping	hydraulic, double-acting	hydraulic, double-acting
Rear forks	trailing link	trailing link
damping	hydraulic	hydraulic
Front brake type	drum 2LS	drum 2LS
diameter mm (in)	200 ($7\frac{3}{4}$)	200 ($7\frac{3}{4}$)
Rear brake type	drum SLS	drum SLS
Tyres	3.50 x 18	3.50 x 18S
Fuel tank capacity in litres (Imp gallons)	17 ($3\frac{3}{4}$)	17 ($3\frac{3}{4}$)
Weight, kg (lb)	202 (445)	202 (445)
Maximum speed km/h (mph)	165 (102)	175 (108)
Frame number range	652001-654955	655004-666320
Engine number range	652001-654955	622001-63000
Number built	2819	11417
Years of production	1955-60	1960-69

* Late US models fitted with 246 gearbox
† Late US models fitted with telescopic front forks

ROAD TESTS

IN announcing their 1961 plans last autumn, BMWs virtually claimed to have achieved the impossible—that is, to have improved both the pep and refinement of a a range of machines long outstanding for advanced design and superb engineering. To have improved either performance or manners without sacrifice of the other—well, difficult though that seemed, maybe the BMW engineers had succeeded. But to better both qualities—that would be believed when it was proved, so far above average was the blend already.

Proof beyond question comes from an extended test of an R69S, the latest version of the sporting six-hundred flat-twin. With a performance to match that of any roadster in production—and, because of the engine's uncanny smoothness, certainly the most usable—the R69S could perhaps be excused some slight sacrifice of the ultimate polish in traditional BMW manners. But no excuse is required.

Wind open the twistgrip and you are whisked along at 100 mph while remaining normally seated. Roll back the grip and the machine will tick-tock sweetly along at 11 mph in top gear without a murmur. Select bottom gear and you can get off and walk alongside with never a thought of reaching for the clutch lever.

No matter how zestfully the R69S is ridden, the exhaust remains incredibly quiet—inaudible to the rider, in fact, and but a whisper to bystanders. Mechanical sound is confined to a faint chatter from the transmission during cold idling. Indeed, so slight a concession does the R69S make to its voracious appetite for road burning that one has to split hairs to record it:

THERE is no more strain in sustaining 100 mph than 50 mph.

The most aristocratic of thoroughbreds

whereas on the 494 cc R50 tested by *The Motor Cycle* in 1955 the rider could hear the faint hum of the front tyre above any other noise at 40 mph in top gear, it proved necessary on the R69S to rise off the seat and lean forward to hear the tyre! In other words, for unobtrusiveness and tractability the R69S is bettered—and that infinitesimally only by lower-compression BMW twins.

The term "cruising speed" loses its significance. All speeds from a dawdle to maximum proved supremely pleasant and comfortable. Times without number 100 mph was held with the rider sitting upright, while 110 mph was occasionally reached downhill. In the face of a strong headwind long upgrades were surmounted at 85 to 90

mph. Whatever the conditions the transverse cylinder layout kept the engine abnormally cool. Calibrated in kph (the test model was equipped for use in Germany), the speedometer was as near accurate as makes no difference.

In adverse conditions, the secret of getting the best out of the BMW is to hold third gear up to a speed of 90 mph, which is reached remarkably quickly. And so smooth and quiet is the engine even at peak revs that once or twice 100 mph was inadvertently touched in third—well into the valve-float range but without adverse effect.

Quite literally there is no more strain in sustaining 100 mph than 50 mph. The slight forward set of the handlebar and rearward set of the footrests

It glides through the streets with the grace of a Rolls Royce

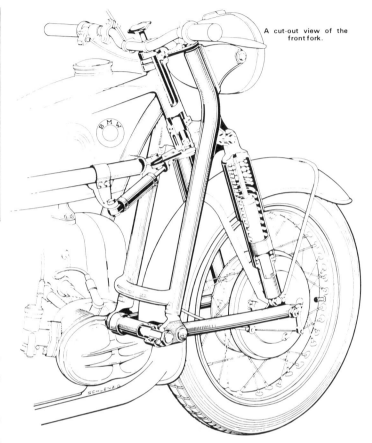

A cut-out view of the front fork.

provides just enough forward lean to make it unnecessary to pull hard on the bar in resisting wind pressure. No noise but the rush of wind assails the rider's ears and there is not the faintest trace of vibration—thanks to the opposed arrangement of the cylinders.

Perfect balance prevents any wheel or fork flutter while the springing, a trifle firm at low speeds, is extraordinarily well damped and gives superb roadholding. (Incidentally no spanner is required to adjust the preload on the rear springs for pillion riding.)

Rock-steady at all times, the steering, too, contributes enormously to the rider's peace of mind. On wet roads raked by fierce gusty cross-winds that had some machines and cars behaving skittishly the R69S felt as stable as if it were on rails; when the going was icy it responded perfectly to the appropriate delicate riding technique.

Maybe in clubman racing on a vicious circuit conditions might be met to warrant use of the ingenious hydraulic steering damper; but certainly 2,000-odd miles of hard riding on main and secondary roads failed to make it seem remotely desirable to bring it into action. On bends of all sorts the BMW could be heeled hard over with every confidence; measuring only 21 in across, the footrests never grounded.

In spite of its suitability for ultra-fast cruising the riding position could not be faulted for town threading. In any case the range of adjustments is above average. For instance, besides providing for swivelling, the handlebar clamps have alternative mounting holes in the fork yoke. And the pillion footrests, as well as those for the rider, are adjustable for position. Excellently shaped, the twin-seat is not merely comfortable—it is luxurious; and with a length of 28 in it provides ample room for two.

None of the controls could be better placed and all of them worked sweetly. At the cost of a full movement of

three-eighths of a turn (instead of the average quarter) the twistgrip gives a variable throttle-opening rate—slow initially and becoming progressively faster. In traffic crawls the slow action is a boon since it makes ultra-delicate grip twisting unnecessary. Moreover, in effect it combines with the sweet low-speed running and heavy flywheel to conceal the super-sporting potential.

Notwithstanding the high compression ratio (9.5 to 1) little effort was required to spin the engine by means of the transverse kick-starter; for this purpose it was most convenient to stand on the left side of the machine. Short riders found the footpiece a trifle high; but the centre stand gave ample firm support for kick-starting.

Since no strangler or air control is fitted the engine proved fairly sensitive to the throttle setting and carburettor flooding for cold starting when the weather was really wintry. However, once the best drill was determined—moderately generous flooding and twistgrip set as for a fast tickover—a first-kick response was the rule rather than the exception. In milder weather the drill was not so critical provided the pilot air screws were left a shade on the rich side, as set at the factory. With that proviso again, the engine warmed up fairly rapidly to

the stage where throttle response was unhesitant. The auto-advance worked perfectly so that pinking could not be induced; in deference to the high compression ratio, super-premium petrol was used.

Engagement of the single-plate clutch seemed sweeter than on earlier models and quite as smooth as that of any multi-plate layout. With an engine-speed clutch and heavy flywheel, BMWs have never boasted the slickest of gear changes. Because of the closer spacing of the ratios, that on the R69S is the best of the bunch; and though there may be sweeter changes it is well up to average.

When changing up the best results were obtained by first applying a moderate upward pressure to the pedal so that the dog clutches slipped home as soon as the clutch lever and twistgrip were eased. An appreciable blip of the throttle paid off when changing down. With the engine idling in its customary slow and dependable fashion, bottom gear usually went into engagement without a sound. Marked by a green light glowing in the headlamp shell, neutral was easy to locate.

Equal to any emergency and thoroughly waterproof, the brakes could bring squeals from both tyres at top speed, yet were smooth and progress-

SPARKING plugs, valve covers and carburettors are extremely accessible. Both cylinders breathe through a large air filter. For the transverse kick-starter there is a rubber limit stop on the lower frame tube.

The iron fist in a velvet glove

INFORMATION PANEL

ENGINE: BMW 595 cc (72 × 73 mm) overhead-valve, horizontally opposed twin with needle-roller rocker bearings. Crankshaft supported in ball and roller bearings; roller big-end bearings. Aluminium-alloy cylinder heads. Compression ratio, 9.5 to 1. Wet-sump lubrication; sump capacity, 4 pints.
CARBURETTORS: Bing with progressive-rate twin-pull twistgrip. Air filter.
IGNITION and LIGHTING: Noris rotating-magnet magneto with auto-advance, and separate Noris 60/90-watt dynamo both enclosed by crankcase front cover. Varta 6-volt, 8-ampere-hour battery. Bosch 6½-in-diameter headlamp with pre-focus light unit and 35/35-watt main bulb Detachable ignition and lighting switch.
TRANSMISSION: BMW four-speed gear box in unit with engine; positive-stop foot control. Gear ratios: bottom, 13.03 to 1; second, 8.53 to 1; third, 6.07 to 1; top, 4.82 to 1. Single-plate dry clutch in engine flywheel. Final drive by enclosed shaft and helical bevel gears. Engine r.p.m. at 30 mph in top gear, 1,915.
FUEL CAPACITY: 3¾ gallons.
TYRES: Continental 3.50 × 18 in front and rear.
BRAKES: Both approximately 8 in diameter × 1¼ in wide; twin leading shoe front; finger adjusters.
SUSPENSION: BMW pivoted front and rear forks controlled by multi-rate spring and hydraulic units. Manual two-position adjustment for load on rear units. Two-position fork-trail and load adjustments at front.
WHEELBASE: 55½ in unladen. Ground clearance, 6½ in unladen.
SEAT: BMW twin-seat; unladen height: 31 in.
WEIGHT: 450 lb fully equipped and with

full oil sump and approximately one gallon of petrol.
PRICE: £440; with purchase tax (in Great Britain only), £530 15s.
ROAD TAX: £3 15s a year; £1 7s for four months.
MAKERS: Bayerische Motoren Werke, AG., München, Germany.
BRITISH CONCESSIONAIRES: A.F.N., Ltd., Falcon Works, London Road, Isleworth, Middlesex.

PERFORMANCE DATA
(Obtained at the Motor Industry Research Association's proving ground, Lindley.)

MEAN MAXIMUM SPEED:	
Bottom:	*45 mph
Second:	*68 mph
Third:	*95 mph
Top:	104 mph

*Valve float occurring.
HIGHEST ONE-WAY SPEED: 108 mph (conditions: very strong side wind; rider wearing two-piece plastic suit and overboots).

MEAN ACCELERATION	10-30 m ph	20-40 m ph	30-50 m ph
Bottom	2.5 sec	2.5 sec	—
Second	3.6 sec	3.4 sec	3.0 sec
Third	5.2 sec	4.1 sec	3.8 sec
Top	—	6.6 sec	5.2 sec

Mean speed at end of quarter-mile from rest: 88 mph. Mean time to cover standing quarter-mile: 15 sec.
PETROL CONSUMPTION: At 30 mph 100 mpg; at 40 mph 90 mpg; at 50 mph 75 mpg; at 60 mph 66 mpg.
BRAKING: From 30 mph to rest, 28 feet (surface, dry tarmac).
TURNING CIRCLE: 16 ft.
MINIMUM NON-SNATCH SPEED: 11 mph in top gear.
WEIGHT PER CC: 0.76 lb.

ive enough to give every confidence on slippery surfaces.

Rubber mounted, the headlamp threw a wide, far-reaching driving beam quite adequate for speeds of 80 mph and more. The horn, too, did what it should, i.e. gave clear and unmistakable warning of approach, though for really fast riding the thumb-operated main-beam flasher was a most effective substitute.

To comply with a new German law, the BMW has winking direction indicators at the handlebar ends; they proved a great convenience and the firm neutral location of the operating switch prevents overshooting that position when cancelling. The horn button and dip switch on the left and the headlamp flasher and winking switch on the right can all be operated merely by swivelling the thumbs.

As to maintenance, that calls for considerable revision of accepted ideas. No oil is required between changes; and though valve clearances and contact-breaker gap are so accessible as to invite inspection, once the engine is run-in checking between decokes is likely to be a waste of time. Transmission maintenance amounts to no more than changing 150 cc of oil in both bevel housing and shaft tube, and just under 1¼ pints in the gear box, every 7,500 miles—a fair period for chain renewal on an orthodox model driven the way the R69S can be. Even the tyres on the test model lost no pressure in two months.

As a roadster the R69S is incomparable—the most aristocratic of thoroughbreds. Equally at home gliding through packed city streets with the grace of a Rolls Royce or whispering majestically along at 100 mph it conceals its iron fist in a velvet glove. To ride it is to appreciate new levels of satisfaction and pride, to understand why connoisseurs who can afford it are prepared to pay a very high price, and to envy the West German enthusiast who can buy it for the equivalent of about £340.

The 590 c.c. Horizontally-opposed Twin o.h.v.

B.M.W. "R69"

The Fatherland's Biggest and Most Up-to-date Production Machine Tested by "Motor Cycling"

OF all German machines, the undoubted leader in both technical design and detail finish is the B.M.W. R69 which, being a 590 c.c. o.h.v. twin, is one of the few Continental designs which can provide a direct comparison with the many big British models. However, though the B.M.W. may therefore be considered as probably the nearest equivalent to our popular 600 and 650 c.c. vertical twins, several reservations should be entered. One is that it is designed as a luxury tourer, not as a sports machine. Such features as the now almost traditional h.o. engine and shaft drive make exact analogy with chain-drive vertical twins almost impossible, the design philosophy underlying the two schools of thought being entirely different, while one could buy two British twins for the price of one B.M.W., and still have the price of a puncture outfit to spare!

The safest ground from which a tester can judge the latest in a long line of Munich-built flat twins is in comparison with earlier models of the same marque. There can be no doubt that, with its swinging-fork front and rear suspension and fully enclosed transmission, the new B.M.W. is a vast improvement over its predecessors, which themselves held an enviable reputation. The rear suspension system is, of course, unconventional, the spring units being clamped into position at about their half-way point; and angular movement accommodated within the unit itself. The frame, too, more nearly

resembles an old-type "loop" structure, but it offers great rigidity, and a solid anchorage for a sidecar.

On taking over the test R69—kindly loaned for the occasion by private owner Bill Potter, of Thornton Heath, Surrey—our man's first mental note was that the 600 c.c. engine was slightly noisier, mechanically, than had been the previous 500 c.c. job. That is to say one could, by listening really hard, just hear the valve gear in action! That frou-frou rustle apart, there was not a single mechanical sound audible.

Clutch action was smooth and sweet, the gear change—provided the rider's tactics were adapted to suit an engine-speed clutch —positive and easy. At first, the riding position gave signs of being just a little different from that to which a British rider would normally be accustomed. One is seated a little more to the rear—a result of the transverse engine. It took only a few miles, however, to become enthusiastic over the natural attitude provided by the B.M.W.,

and it was with amazement that a tester normally finicky over control co-relationships, discovered, after nearly 1,000 miles of riding, that the footrests were staggered by a couple of inches to suit the equivalent arrangement of the two big "pots."

The riding comfort provided by a combination of sprung saddle and suspension impossible to fault was a revelation. With one possible exception, the R 69 is the best-sprung machine in the rider's longish experience. Since the front end is made under Earles' licence, part of the credit obviously belongs to Birmingham! Readily adjustable by means of a built-in tommy bar on each leg, the rear springing harmonized well with the front, giving superb road-holding under all conditions.

Though flexible enough to allow of 20 m.p.h. traffic negotiation in top gear, the big engine really revelled under open road conditions. There seemed no limit on one's cruising speed. "Poodling" at a touring 40 m.p.h., or hurtling along the highway at

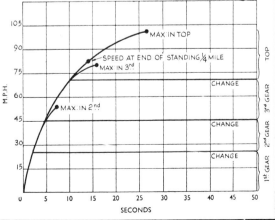

TESTER'S ROAD REPORT

Maximum Speeds in :—

Time from Standing Start

Top Gear (Ratio 4.9 to 1) 102 m.p.h. 6,760 r.p.m. 26.6 secs.

Third Gear (Ratio 7.8 to 1) 81 m.p.h. 8,300 r.p.m. 15.2 secs.

Second Gear (Ratio 9.6 to 1) 54 m.p.h. 7,020 r.p.m. 7 secs.

Speeds over measured Quarter Mile :—

Flying Start 100 m.p.h.   Standing Start 61 m.p.h.

Braking Figures On DRY TARMACADAM **Surface, from 30 m.p.h. :—**

Both Brakes 20 ft.   Front Brake 26 ft.   Rear Brake 64 ft.

Fuel Consumption :—

30 m.p.h. 90 m.p.g.   40 m.p.h. 76 m.p.g.   50 m.p.h. 68 m.p.g.

(Graph: M.P.H. vs SECONDS, with points labelled MAX IN TOP, SPEED AT END OF STANDING ¼ MILE, MAX IN 3rd, MAX IN 2nd; gear columns showing 1st GEAR, 2nd GEAR, 3rd GEAR, TOP with CHANGE markers)

(Above) This view of the very clean engine unit shows the built-in air filter and the accessibility of the carburetter and rocker-box cover.

(Right) The Earles-type front forks and the extremely powerful twin-leading-shoe front brake.

MOTOR CYCLING SPORTS MODEL ROAD TESTS

Without artificial "styling," the R69 presents a very business-like appearance.

over "90" per—it was all the same to the R69. Seldom has the tester straddled a machine which made high-speed cruising so ridiculously easy! At 85-90 m.p.h., with the suspension smoothing out the bumps, the engine vibrationless, and the exhaust note a steady drone, nothing but the whistling of the wind and the needle of the speedometer indicated one's speed. It was just like riding in a big, comfortable car.

Acceleration—though not startling—was more than adequate for all practical purposes, the power coming in smoothly, without a flat spot, all the way up the range. Once the knack had been learned, quick gear changes could be made in either direction.

Steering was also first rate. Thanks to a low centre of gravity, the R69 could be put into corners on any line the rider cared to

choose, and it would hold to it tenaciously. It could be rapidly warped over from side to side—thanks in no small measure to an ideal riding position which enabled full knee pressure to be brought to bear—and was as handy as a lightweight when it came to manœuvring through traffic.

With such attributes, it was not surprising that the tester came to regard it as an ideal machine for putting up averages. On one memorable morning, when Press schedules were tight and time short, the R69 conveyed a staffman from mid-Sussex to the New Forest and back between breakfast-time and lunch, with an hour or so's work thrown in! Over this tricky cross-country journey, measuring just over 90 miles on each stretch, the R69 responded nobly, doing what had to be done in the minimum time, but also

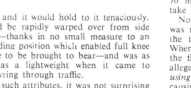

The new swinging fork rear suspension, with enclosed drive shaft and adjustable spring unit.

with the maximum safety. Naturally, his required the best use to be made of the model's ability to cruise well up the scale, and it was frequently held with the needle at around the 90 m.p.h. mark, with occasional downhill sprints bringing it near to 100 m.p.h. Under such conditions, fuel consumption naturally rose, but normally an overall 70 m.p.g. could be expected on give-and-take going.

No small contribution to the R69's appeal was made by its excellent brakes. That at the front was of two-leading-shoe design. When the test figures were being carried out, the first two stops were both made in the allegedly "can't be done" distance of 26 ft. *using the front brake alone!* For fear of causing apoplexy amongst readers, attempts were thereupon discontinued. With both brakes in action, the best figure ever obtained in a *Motor Cycling* test—20 ft. from a corrected 30 m.p.h. (the speedo. was 10% fast)—was obtained on the two first tries. No more were made.

Oil Tightness

On other points, too, the machine earned full marks. The lighting was first-rate; oil-tightness as near absolute as made no difference; the silencing effective; subsidiary design neat; mudguarding good. A hyper-critical tester might have complained that the dipswitch was a little too far from the left hand for comfort; that the otherwise neat toolbox, with Yale-type lock, concealed behind the left knee-rest was the Devil's own delight to repack; and that no adjustment appeared to be provided for a gear pedal which—to be honest—didn't in this case need readjustment, anyway.

But beyond those minor points of detail design, nothing adverse could be said—and certainly they count for little compared with the overall excellence of the layout, handling, performance and finish of this "100 m.p.h. plus" scion of a long line of foreign aristocrats. For a price of nearly £500 one expects a motorcycle of nearly Rolls-Royce quality. It is to its manufacturer's credit that the B.M.W. R69 provides it.

BRIEF SPECIFICATION

Engine: 590 c.c. B.M.W. horizontally-opposed o.h.v. twin four-stroke; bore 72 mm. by stroke 73 mm.=590 c.c.; cast iron cylinders; light alloy heads; valves pushrod operated; C.R. 8 to 1; Claimed b.h.p. 35/6,800 r.p.m.; Bing carburetters.

Transmission: Four-speed gearbox bolted-up to engine; car-type clutch; ratios 4.9, 7.8, 9.6 and 16.95 to 1; direct primary drive; final drive by enclosed shaft to hypoid gears.

Frame: Of welded tubular construction; duplex main frame, with extended 'oop-type rear bearers.

Wheels: Light alloy rims carry Continental 3.50-in. by 18-in. tyres.

Brakes: 7.9-in. twin-leading-shoe front; 7.9-in. rear.

Lubrication: By gear pump submerged in engine sump.

Electrical Equipment: 6-volt 60-watt generator, crankshaft driven, supplies current for battery; head lamp; tail lamp; horn; ignition and neutral warning lights; combined horn button and dip-switch control unit.

Suspension: B.M.W. front forks, built under Earles licence, with B.M.W. hydraulically damped suspension units. Swinging-fork rear suspension with adjustable B.M.W. hydraulically damped suspension units.

Tank: Of welded steel, 4 gallons capacity. Locking tool box hidden beneath left knee-grip.

Dimensions: Wheelbase, 55¼ in.; ground clearance, 5 in.; unladen seat height, 28½ in.; dry weight, 445 lb.

Finish: Black enamel with white lining; B.M.W. motif in blue and white on tank, chromium-plated details.

General Equipment: Comprehensive tool kit; tyre inflator; puncture repair outfit; steering head lock; tool box lock; 120 m.p.h. VDO speedometer mounted in head-lamp shell.

Price: £397 plus £95 5s. 7d. P.T.=£492 5s. 7d.

Annual Tax: £3 15s.; quarterly £1 0s. 8d.

Makers: Bayerische Motoren Werke A G, Lerchenauerstrasse 76, Munich, Germany.

Concessionnaires: A.F.N., Ltd., Falcon Works, London Road, Isleworth, Hounslow, Middx.

OWNER'S VIEW

Roy Harper's first interview was with Fred Secker, President of the BMW Club.

RH: Why were you interested in the R69?
FS: I liked the R69 compared with the 60, for example, because it was that much stronger with much more poke.
RH: When and why did you buy your R69?
FS: I had friends in Germany who introduced me to BMWs. Later, I came across an R69 sitting in Bill Slocombe's showroom. He suggested a figure and I replied that the bike would be sitting there for a long time! Anyway, a while later, Bill offered it to me at a reduced price and I bought it.
RH: What condition was the bike in?
FS: Good.
RH: Did the bike need much repair during your ownership?
FS: Very little. I owned the bike for three years and travelled 47,000 miles including extensive tours on the continent. A new rear main bearing was fitted and I replaced valves and guides, etc. but did not have to spend much on the bike. It was very economic to run but became quite thirsty when I was cruising above 90 mph.
RH: Any difficulties obtaining spares?
FS: No. No problem at all.

RH: What kind of handling and performance did the R69 have?
FS: I'd load the bike up with luggage and take my wife to the Elephant Rally, for example. The bike would cruise all day in the nineties, without any fuss.
RH: Was the bike in everyday use?
FS: I used to travel to and from work. Riding through London I averaged around 50 mpg.
RH: Did you win any prizes in concours events?
FS: No. I bought it for use, not for show.
RH: Did you compete in any trials or races?
FS: No. I used it for touring, not racing.
RH: How long have you been President of the BMW Club?
FS: I've been Secretary or President for nineteen years. The Club means a great deal to me.
RH: Is interest in the R69 increasing?
FS: When I put mine up for sale, I advertised it in one of the weeklies and had about 300 replies altogether. I sold it for more than I paid for it. A friend of mine has a brand new R69S ... never been used, never been registered! and he has been offered £4,000 for it! So that indicates the interest.
RH: Any unusual incidents?
FS: I was once pulled up by a policeman on the North Circular Road. I'd seen him in the mirror ... he said, 'Can you tell me the number of your bike?' I said, 'Yes, it's YCR 14.' 'I stopped you,' he explained, 'because your registration lettering is the one used in the town where I come from. I didn't think a bike could be in such good condition for that year.'

We had a long chat and finally I said, 'You'd better give me a note for my boss to explain why I've been held up!'

I had an odd fault after returning through Belgium from the Cologne Show. I was getting a wobble at about 20 mph. Car horns blared and lights flashed. Anyway, when I examined the bike and

looked at the leading links of the front forks I discovered that salt had got in and had caused sticking, resulting in insufficient movement.
RH: How would you sum up the enjoyment from ownership?
FS: I had so much pleasure from it. I could ride along with a full load and the bike would get me there without trouble and without tiring me, unlike some Japanese bikes which seem to cause fatigue in the rider. I now own an R100S which is ideal.
RH: What advice would you give to anyone contemplating buying an R69 today?
FS: If I were buying an R69 today, I would look at the back of the gearbox where the clutch goes in; there's a little tray and I'd look for oil in it; and if there's no oil, that's good. And I'd look for oil seep round the crankcase and the timing cover. And that's about all.

The author next interviewed Ted Davis, the former chief tester of the Vincent HRD Company and now a member of the BMW Club. During the past 20 years Ted has owned an R50, R69S, R90S, R100RS, R60 & R65.
RH: What was the attraction of the R69S?
TD: Better performance than the other BMWs of that era. More horse power. It's different from any other bike.
RH: When and why did you buy your R69S?
TD: 1974. I was interested in the Earles forks.
RH: What condition was it in?
TD: Good. No work was necessary. (The silencers tended to rot away and were replaced with stainless steel silencers.)
RH: Any problems getting parts?
TD: No, but they are expensive.
RH: What were the handling and performance like?
TD: Handling was cumbersome. Performance was moderate. Gear changing was slow. The heavy flywheels worked against quick changes. The hydraulic damper felt peculiar.
RH: Was your 69 in everyday use?

TD: I bought it for touring. It would cruise at 80 to 90 mph along the autobahn and return about 50 mpg.
RH: Do you belong to the BMW Club?
TD: Yes. It's very helpful and useful.
RH: Did you enter the bike in any concours events or races?
TD: No. I bought it for road use.
RH: Was there a specialist whom you found useful?
TD: Yes. Bryants of Biggleswade.
RH: How did the unique throttle control respond when you were flicking through the bends.
TD: When you ride an R69 you don't flick through the bends.
RH: Did you suffer from the wobbles that afflicted the BMWs a few years ago?
TD: You're thinking of the R75 which unseated one or two policemen. I saw police bikes with wrong fairings, and tyre pressures. The rear units were susceptible to their settings. I saw police bikes with different settings each side!
RH: How would you sum up your enjoyment of the R69S?
TD: You know you will get there without trouble or fatigue.
RH: What advice would you give to any one contemplating purchase?
TD: Buy one with a low mileage.

Roy Harper's final interview was with Margaret Clarke, who owns an R69S.
RH: Why are you so interested in the R69S?
MC: My husband, Bruce, owned a BMW for several years and I enjoyed riding pillion. He now owns an R100S but I'm not tall enough to straddle it comfortably. I prefer the R69S with its lower saddle.
RH: When and why did you buy your R69S?
MC: I like the older bikes so when, by chance, I had the opportunity of purchasing an R69S a couple of years ago, I bought it and rode it.
RH: What condition was it in?
MC: It wasn't concours but it was roadworthy – in quite good order.
RH: What repair or renovation has been done?
MC: I haven't done much in the

way of repairs. Bruce and I do our own servicing, partly because it's expensive to take a BMW to a service agent (it costs nearly £100 to have a new BMW serviced) and partly because we know the job will have been done properly.

I had a problem with the centre stand. I could manage to put the bike on to the stand but couldn't get it off! So a prop-stand was fitted, which looked a bit unsightly but it was very efficient.

If you can do your own overhauls it's economic to buy an R69 that needs some attention. If you cannot, it's best to buy one in good condition.
RH: Have you experienced any difficulty in obtaining parts?
MC: No, but they are pricey. New exhaust pipes cost around £60. The standard silencer rots away. It's best to replace it with a stainless steel silencer which lasts much longer. Most spares are in stock from UK dealers or they can be bought direct from Germany. The works still produce spares for the older BMWs. (Unlike the Japanese manufacturers who produce so many different models each year and are usually unable to supply owners with parts for even recently made motorcycles.)
RH: What kind of performance and handling does the R69S have?
MC: I like the handling. The R69S doesn't accelerate like a modern BMW, of course, but it can cruise all day at 70 to 80 mph and give 50 to 60 mpg. (The R100S gives around 45 to 50 mpg with a higher cruising speed.)
RH: Is your R69S in regular use?
MC: Not at the moment.
RH: Has your R69S won any prizes in concours events?
MC: No. I cannot afford to bring it up to concours standard even if I

wished to. Once a BMW has been done up it will last for many miles of trouble-free touring.
RH: Do you enter your bike in any rallies or races.
MC: No. It was designed as a high-speed roadster and that is how I prefer it.
RH: Are you a member of the BMW Club?
MC: Yes. Members are very helpful with advice and spares; and the social events are very enjoyable, especially camping week-ends.
RH: Is there a specialist whom you have found particularly useful?
MC: No. As stated, we prefer to do our own maintenance. Last year we took off the head of the 100S to replace the gasket, a job we would shy off doing on a Japanese bike.
RH: How would you sum up the enjoyment you get from your R69S?
MC: I like the tractability of the engine and the simplicity of it. I have taken Bruce on the pillion–he once broke his collar bone and couldn't handle his machine–but I prefer riding solo. I'm light but with the added weight of a passenger I find the bike harder to handle. I do, however, prefer a dualseat to the single saddle – it's more practical.
RH: What advice would you give to a potential owner of the R69S?
MC: It's a good idea to take a BMW owner along to check over the bike you're thinking of buying. It takes a while to get used to the gearbox but in time you learn to make a clonk-free gearchange!

BUYING

Only one variation of the R69 was produced, the R69S which appeared in 1960. Enthusiasts prefer the faster R69S which has more power than the R69 without any great loss of fuel economy. Conversely, the R69 is a much rarer animal, production being about a quarter of the number made of the R69S, and might therefore be of more interest to the collector.

Demand for these models from the 'Earles era' is steadily growing and no doubt will continue so to do.

The value of a machine sometimes depends upon such practical considerations as the availability of parts. Spares seem to be plentiful at the moment and many are common to all the 500 and 600 cc models in the 'Earles' range. (The bikes are reliable and rarely need replacements, anyway.)

Another aspect of the price is the difficulty and cost of getting insurance. Several firms will offer a guaranteed value, i.e. they will pay the full amount agreed between the owner of a BMW and themselves in the event of theft or total write-off from fire.

There aren't really any problem areas, although the standard silencer does tend to rot due to the retention of moisture.

The engine is well and truly cooled (especially the cylinders hanging out in the air stream) and it runs at a temperature too low to cause evaporation of the offending moisture lurking in the silencers, which consequently deteriorate fairly rapidly. Stainless steel silencers are more expensive initially but are cheaper over a lengthy period as they last so much longer.

Another problem can arise from sludge forming in the engine and causing big-end failure. Bruce Preston, explained the nature of the problem. 'You know how the system for lubricating the big-ends works? Oil from each main bearing housing enters a channel in a disc plate mounted on the crankshaft (one either side of the big-ends). Centrifugal force throws the oil around into the big-ends. If sludge forms it could ruin the big-ends. The dilemma is whether to clean out the engine after 30,000 to 40,000 miles or to wait for the big-end to seize.'

A lot of motorcyclists riding lesser makes would like to know that their big-ends would last half that mileage.

Bruce rode R69S models in the 60s and recorded his impressions in *Motorcycle Sport* (March 1968).

What a prospective buyer may not know is that different bikes – though ostensibly the same model – will have different characteristics. Bruce discovered that really fast riders swapped the standard springs in the suspension units for the stronger sidecar ones. One of the bikes Bruce rode sported telescopic forks instead of the standard Earles, a set-up that gave more 'feel' for the fast rider. However, the Earles front-end gave more comfort. There are probably modified R69s around today so *caveat emptor!*

If you intend buying an R69 or R69S take along someone who knows the model. Spares are expensive so it's obviously best to purchase an example that doesn't need any.

The BMW Club has several helpful members with experience of the Earles range so it is a good idea to join. It is also a good idea to buy a bike that has a known history. The BMW owners usually keep a record of maintenance and replacements.

A good R69 will give 80,000 to 100,000 trouble-free miles of enjoyable riding, solo or sidecar. (Ted Davis reckons Earles forks are better for sidecar work than solo.)

There are reputable dealers and there are, well, others; BMW owners will know the goodies and the baddies and can advise accordingly.

Current prices in the UK (1983) are two to three times the original new purchase price.

The big advantage of buying a motorcycle in comparison with a car is that you can *see* the frame parts and check them for rust or damage; and you can *hear* the engine of a Bee-em...well, just!

CLUBS, SPECIALISTS & BOOKS

The BMW owners I know are all hard riders. They travel vast distances across Europe and North America and in 1977 some took their bikes to Canada aboard a jumbo jet as part of a group organised by the Vincent HRD Owners Club.

Clubs

Enthusiasts formed a club in 1951 called The BMW Society of Great Britain but later changed this to The BMW Club.

The Club is open to owners and ex-owners of BMW motor-cycles and has several local sections throughout the world to cater for the local needs of members.

The Club organises dinners, camping week-ends, tours, etc. for its 2,600 members and holds a major event every Bank Holiday.

The Club publishes a monthly magazine which is circulated to all members throughout the world.

For further details, applicants should write to the General Secretary, Fred Secker, 64 Cavalry Drive, March, Cambridgeshire PE15 9EQ, England.

Specialists

The following are known to specialise in BMW motorcycles.

The author cannot be held responsible if any dealer fails to provide a good service.

Dave Dickinson,
Casa Mia
Barbados Hill,
Tintern,
Gwent.
Tel. 02918-344

Allan Jefferies Ltd,
206 Saltaire Road,
Shipley,
Yorkshire.
Tel. 0274 587451

Gus Kuhn Motors Ltd,
275/277 Clapham Road,
London SW9 9BJ.
Tel. 01-733 1002

Roy Pidcock Motorcycles Ltd,
227 Osmaston Road,
Derby DE3 8LD.
Tel. 0332 49673/367947

Hughenden M40 Motorcycles,
Milton Common,
Oxford OX9 2NU.
Tel. 08446 701/2

Books

BMW Twins & Singles by Roy Bacon
The best history of the post-war BMWs
Published by Osprey 1982
Bahnstormer by LJK Setright
History of the bikes up to 1976
Published by Transport Bookman 1977

BMW by Michael Frostick
Pictorial history (mostly of cars)
Includes 62 pictures of motorcycles
Published by Dalton Watson 1976
The Story of BMW Motor Cycles by Robert Croucher
Includes section on dealers
Published by Patrick Stephens 1982
The BMW Story
Published by Phoebus 1979
BMW – Motorrader by Ariel Verlag
Excellent pictorial history (German, French & English captions)
Published by Ariel Verlag 1976
Classic Motor Cycles by Vic Willoughby
Includes good write-up on BMW twins
Published by Hamlyn 1973
BMW by Mike Bishop
Service manual for the Earles range 1955-69
Published by Clymer Publications 1978
Exotic Motorcycles by Vic Willoughby
Good chapter on the BMW outfits in the Isle of Man
Published by Osprey 1982

PHOTO
GALLERY

1.   *Fred Secker checking a sparking plug on his R69*

2. All set for a spin to the South of France.

3. Fred Secker riding his R60 in the White Hart M.C.C. Road Trial.

4

5

4. The R60 is almost indistinguishable from the R69. Its low state of tune (6.5 to 1 C.R.) and maximum rpm of 5,600 (28 bhp) enabled owners to clock up huge mileages without mechanical troubles. (Over 20,000 R60s were sold from 1956 to 1967). Fred Secker is aboard.

5. R69 owned by a girl touring in Holland. Note the protective bars around the headlamp, cylinders and rear light. (Steve Boom)

6. Unusual BMW get-up for racing (Steve Boom).

7. BMW at the 1977 BMF Rally, Donington Park, with 6-gallon Hoske petrol tank.

6

7

8

9

8. The faster R69S (9.5 to 1 C.R.) owned by Frank Cox which produces 42 bhp at 7,000 rpm. In my view, the Earles-fork range is the best looking of all the BMW products.

9. Smooth, sleek, reliable, fast and comfortable. And expensive.

10. A front number plate was originally fitted – as shown by the two domed bolt heads.

10

11

11. The stand normally has a peg fitted to enable the rider to raise the bike into position. This R69S has lost its peg, which left the old foot groping in vain.

12. The neat Earles forks.

12

13. The neat arrangement of curvacious tubes! The small loop was added to the crash bars to provide additional protection for the cylinder head.

14. Petrol cap is aluminium. The handlebars – with crossbar – are optional.

15. The one-piece cast aluminium cover.

13

14

15

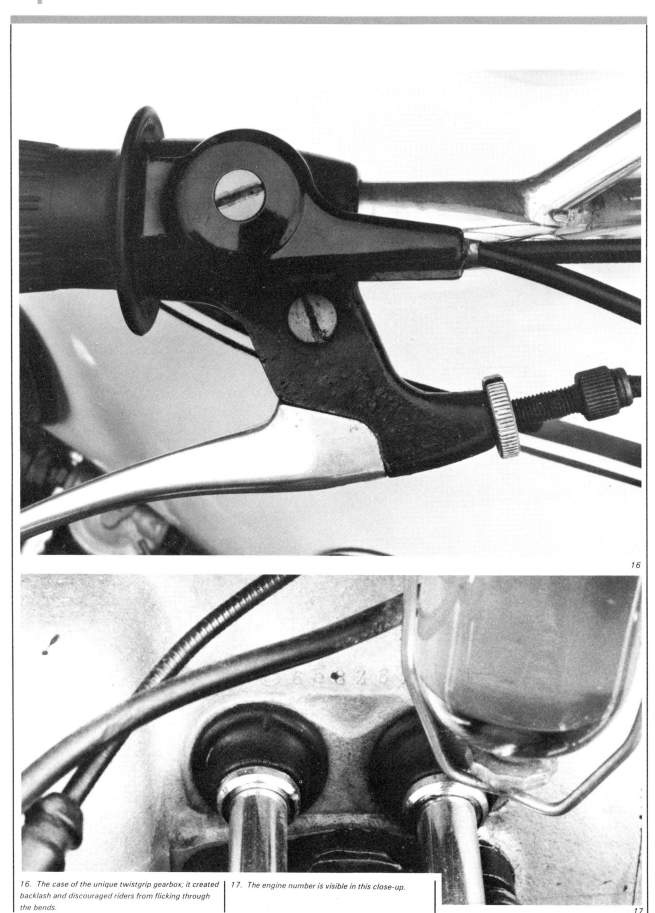

16. The case of the unique twistgrip gearbox; it created backlash and discouraged riders from flicking through the bends.

17. The engine number is visible in this close-up.

16

17

18

18. The handlebar grips are soft and comfortable whereas the ones fitted to my Vincent cause soreness after 200 to 300 miles in the saddle. The adjustment for the clutch cable is clearly shown.

19. The S was added in 1960 to denote the sports version of the R69.

19

20. *The adjustable rear unit. First catch your delectable pillion passenger.*

21. *Not a shoe manufacturer's advertisement but the author's left foot about to prod the kickstart.*

20

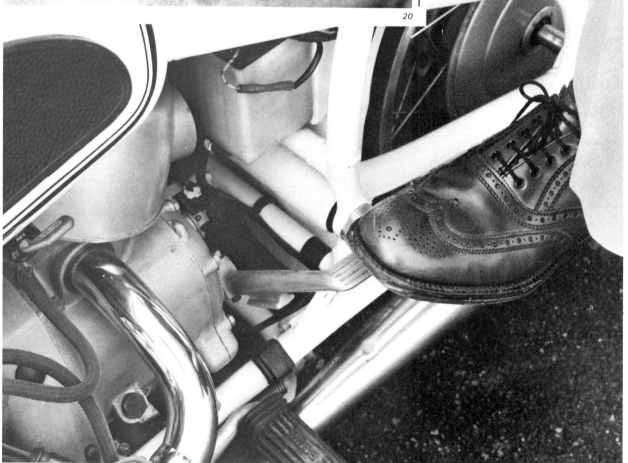

21

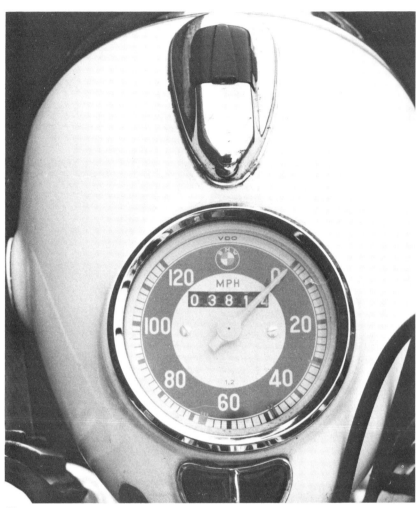

22

23

24

25

22. The speedometer, with ignition lock just above. The latter was sometimes frustrating – I once saw an owner bashing the ignition key with his helmet!

23. Lug for one of the fixing points of a sidecar.

24. Foot brake mounted on right-hand side.

25. The shaft enclosed in the trailing leg on the right-hand side.

26. *Gearchange lever is bottom left and kickstarter position is clearly shown.*

27. *Right-hand view of the effective rear brake.*

26

27

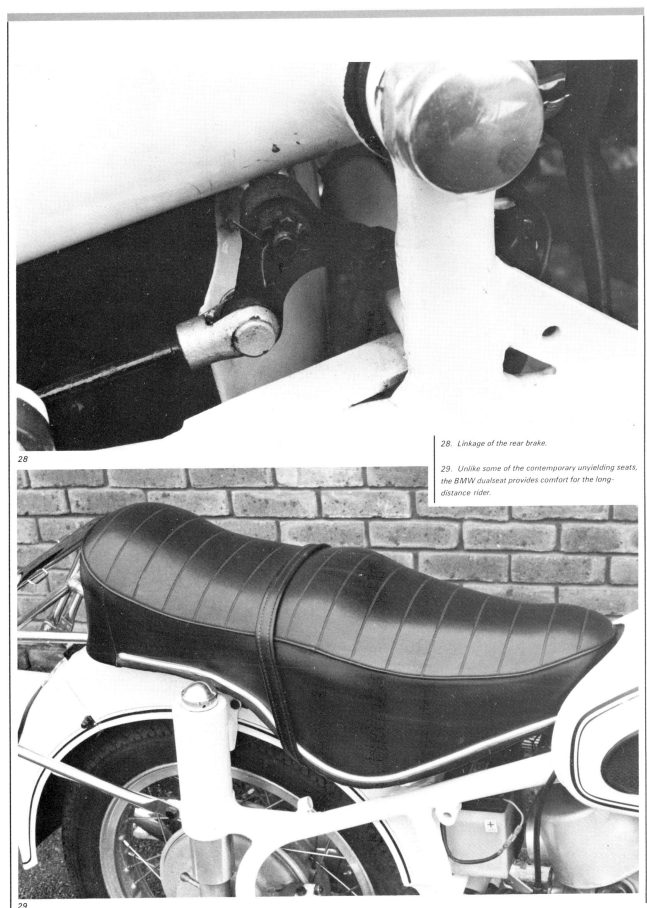

28. Linkage of the rear brake.

29. Unlike some of the contemporary unyielding seats, the BMW dualseat provides comfort for the long-distance rider.

28

29

30. The tidy, unobtrusive pannier frame.

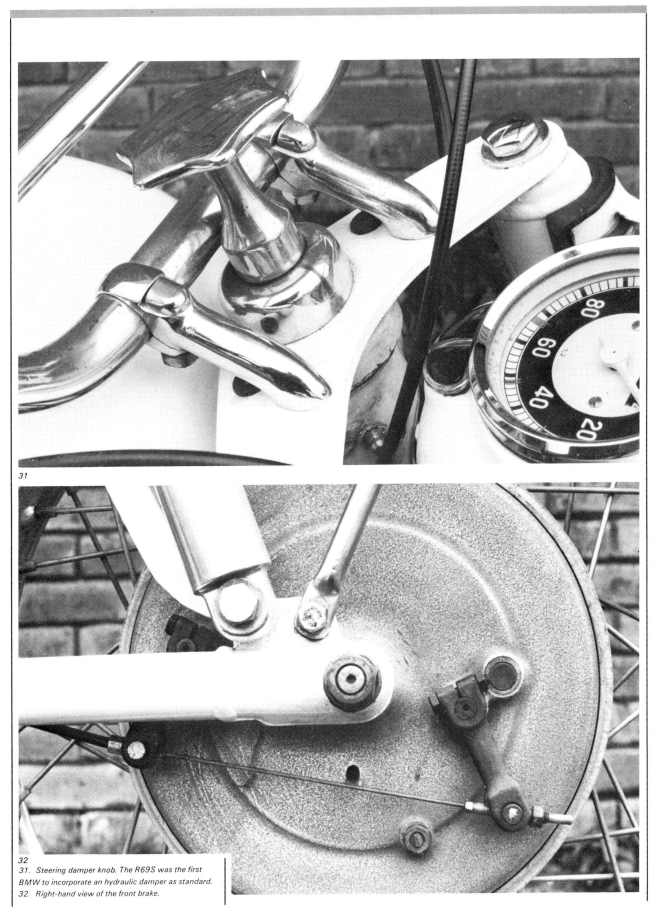

31

32

31. *Steering damper knob. The R69S was the first BMW to incorporate an hydraulic damper as standard.*

32. *Right-hand view of the front brake.*

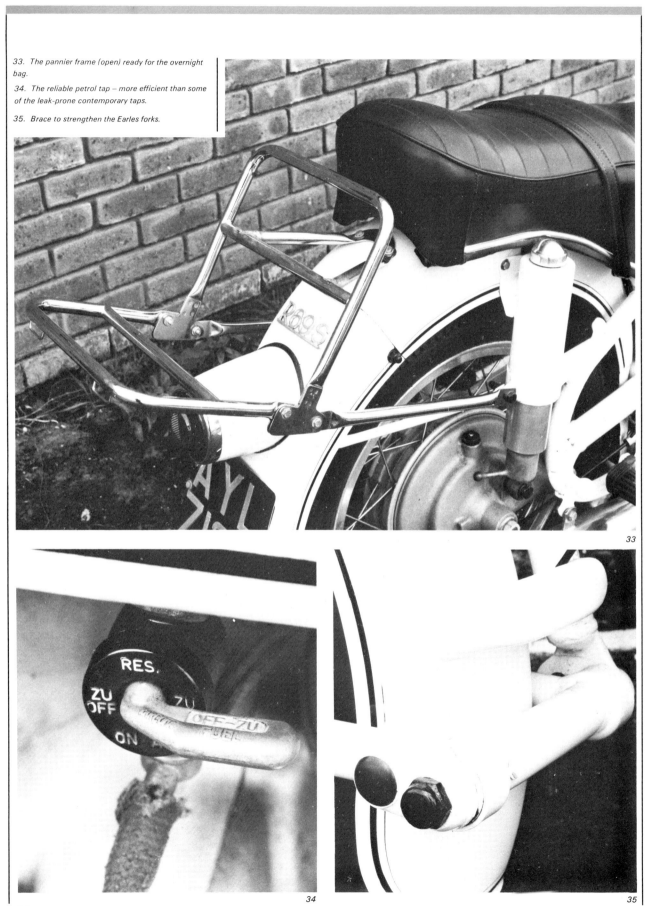

33. The pannier frame (open) ready for the overnight bag.

34. The reliable petrol tap – more efficient than some of the leak-prone contemporary taps.

35. Brace to strengthen the Earles forks.

33

34

35

36

37

36. Rubber gaiter protecting shaft drive.

37. The smart, chromium-plated pannier frame is affixed to the bike by just four bolts (mudguard and rear spring unit).

38. The efficient Everbest *petrol tap*.

39. Alloy rocker cover, alloy head and iron barrel below filter chamber.

40. Not one of the (inverted) saucepans produced by BMW during the forties. This air filter housing has a large aperture at the rear to ensure adequate ingress of air.

41. The distinctive logo shows up more clearly against a white, rather than the usual black, background.

38

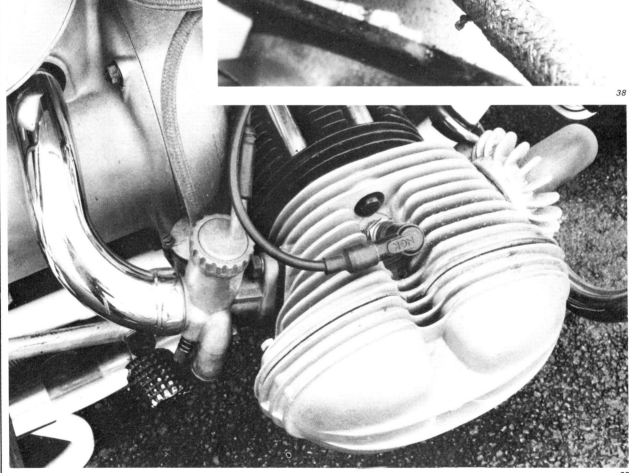

39

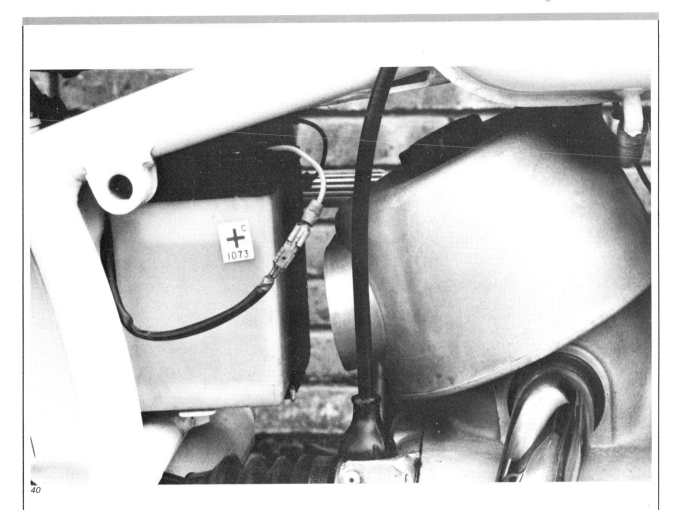

40

41

42. This shot clearly shows the reflector incorporated in the rear light.

43 & 44. Front and rear tyres are 3.50 x 18 inch Continental. Front tyre lasts 20,000 miles; rear tyre lasts 16 to 18,000 miles.

42

43

44

45

46

45. The R69S motif is made from alloy; note the
brackets for straps on the pannier frame.

46. Bing carburettor mounted above the rear brake
pedal on the right hand side of the machine. Note the
accessible position of the adjustment screw.

47. The front brake can be adjusted at the brake arm on the wheel and also by hand at the front brake lever.

48. Gearchange lever on the left-hand side of the R69S.

49. Like a top model, the R69S is photogenic from any angle!

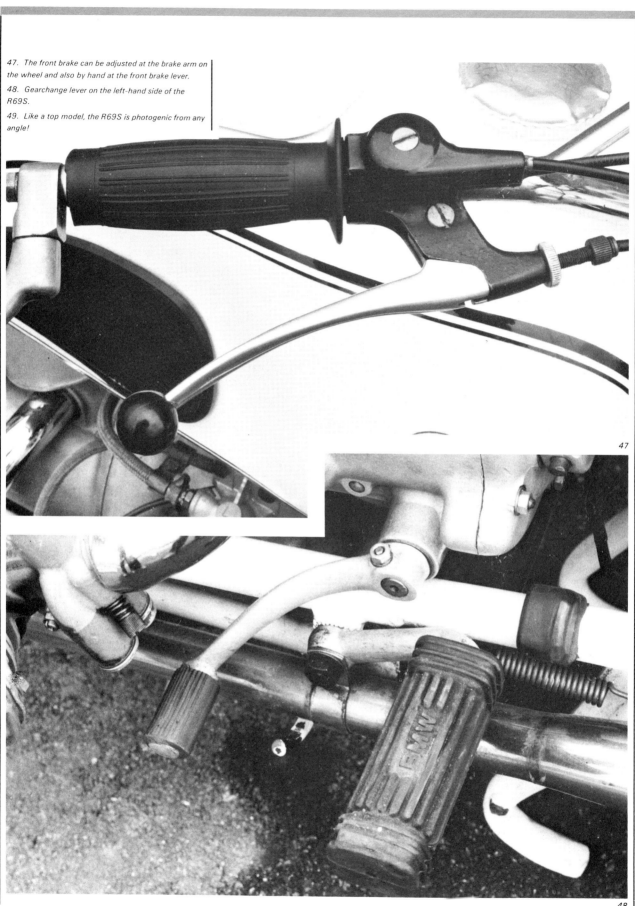

47

48

50. The lug for fitting a sidecar is clearly shown, this being for a right-hand Continental-style sidecar.

51. Left-hand view of front wheel demonstrating width of the effective front-brake.

50

51

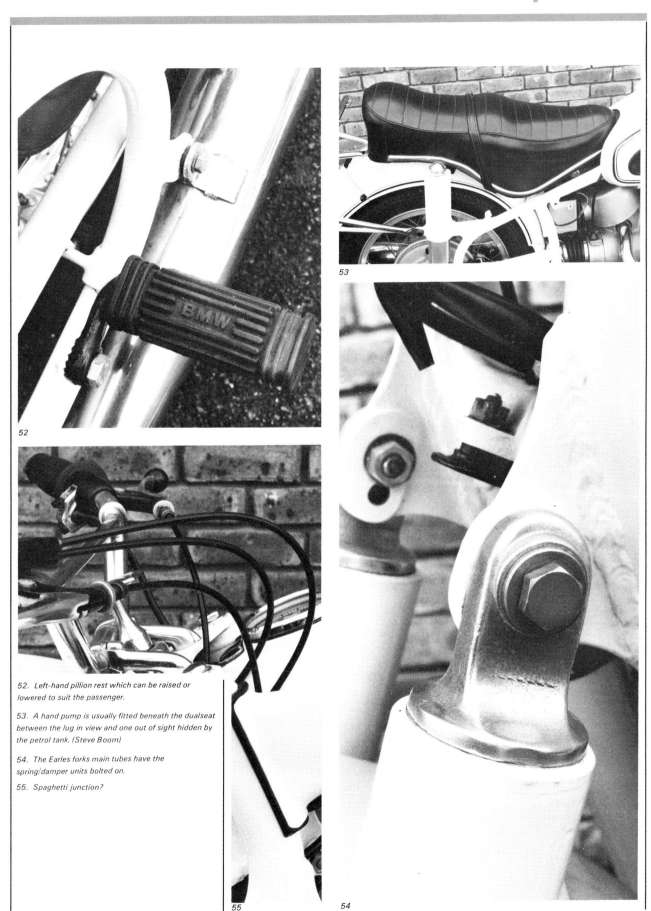

52. Left-hand pillion rest which can be raised or lowered to suit the passenger.

53. A hand pump is usually fitted beneath the dualseat between the lug in view and one out of sight hidden by the petrol tank. (Steve Boom)

54. The Earles forks main tubes have the spring/damper units bolted on.

55. Spaghetti junction?

56. Fairing and pannier frame are non-standard.

57

57. Most R69 models were finished in black.

58. The large petrol tank (an optional extra) for the odd dash across the Continent.

Information Sheet and Application Form

59. Speedometer and rev-counter. The maximum reading of 8,000 rpm emphasizes the low-revving design of the engine.

60. Front cover of the BMW Club's hand-out.

C1

C2

C3

C1, C2, & C3.   Views of an R69S owned by Frank Cox
of Markhouse Motorcycles, Leytonstone. Several
examples of the R69S were finished in white enamel
(which I prefer to the more popular black). Frank runs
the bike on straight oil (Filtrate 40) and frequently tours
on the Continent.

C4

C4. The handlebars and the carrier (open) are optional extras.

C5. Close-up of the rear end (with carrier shut).

C5

C6

C7

C8

C6, & C7.   The seating arrangements give a
comfortable riding position and enable the owner to
cover a large mileage without fatigue.

C8.   The famous badge derived fom BMW's early
aeronautical experience. It is inspired by a pilot's view
through a single-engined aeroplane's propeller.

C9. The smart cover of the ignition switch (whose hygroscopic plunger action often frustrated the owner, let alone a prospective thief!).

C10, & C11. Two views of the Earles forks introduced for 1955.

C9

C10

C11

C12

C13

C12. The model's logo mounted just below the rear mudguard hinge.

C13. The rear light incorporates a reflector.

C14. The 5-gallon petrol tank with knee grip each side – very useful buffers between cold metal and sensitive thighs in chilly weather!

C14

C15.

C16.

C15.   The crash bars have been modified with a small loop added to give additional protection to the cylinder head. The filter bowl on each side of the machine is non-standard.

C16.   Right-hand showing neat installation of engine, gearbox, etc. The starter pedal is on the far right.

C17

C18

C17, & C18.   Most R69S BMWs were finished in black
enamel. This example owned by John Frith has one or
two non-standard items, notably the front fairing carrier.

C19. Right-hand view of the engine.

C20. The fairing provides a suitable mounting place for
the ammeter, whilst the tachometer is attached to the
offside of the front forks.

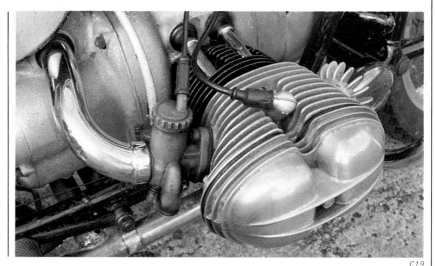

C19

C20